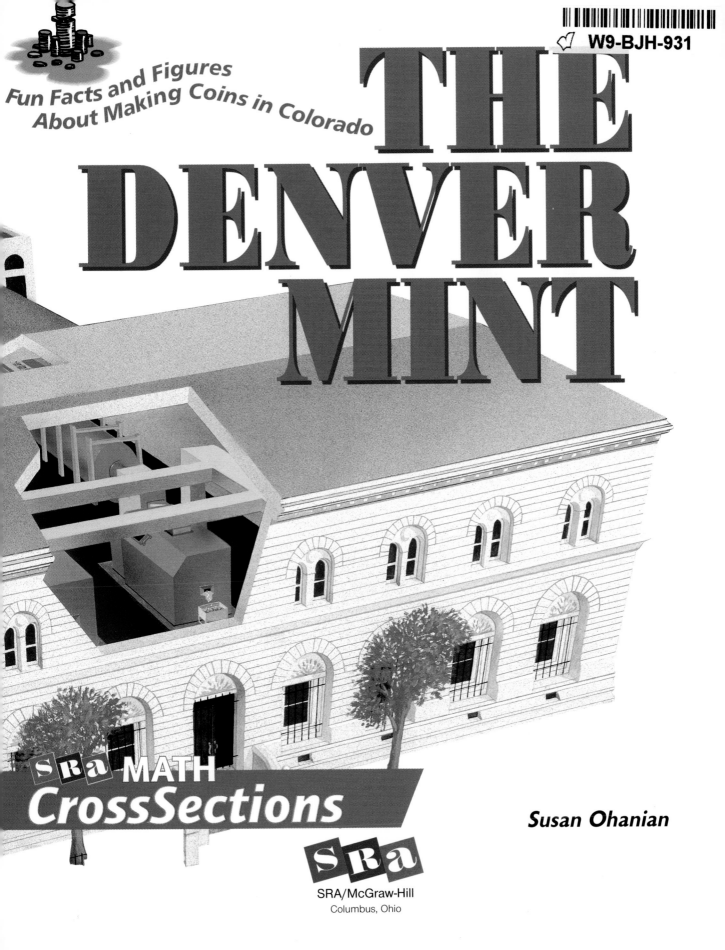

Fun Facts and Figures About Making Coins in Colorado

THE DENVER MINT

SRA MATH
CrossSections

Susan Ohanian

SRA/McGraw-Hill
Columbus, Ohio

Credits

Author

Susan Ohanian

Consultants

Marilyn S. Neil
Professor
Department of Early Childhood
West Georgia College
Carrollton, GA

Thomas A. Romberg
Sears Roebuck Foundation-Bascom
Professor in Education
University of Wisconsin
Madison, WI

Special Thanks to

Robert Hoge, Curator
and Janet Merritt, Museum Manager
American Numismatic Association
Colorado Springs, CO

Michael White
Department of the Treasury
United States Mint
Washington, DC

Send all inquiries to:
SRA/McGraw-Hill
250 Old Wilson Bridge Road
Suite 310
Worthington, OH 43085

Printed in the United States of America.
ISBN 0-02-686717-6
1 2 3 4 5 6 7 8 9 SEG 00 99 98 97 96 95

Reviewers

Paul Douglas Agranoff
1993 Presidential Awardee for Excellence in Science
　and Mathematics
Teaching for Minnesota
St. Francis Elementary School
St. Francis, MN

Christina Carrell Nicolson
1993 Presidential Awardee for Excellence in Science
　and Mathematics
Teaching for Massachusetts
The Pike School
Andover, MA

Sallyjeane H. Stein
1993 Presidential Awardee for Excellence in Science
　and Mathematics
Teaching for New Jersey
Dennis Township Elementary School
Dennisville, NJ

Richard Dale Weir
1993 Presidential Awardee for Excellence in Science
　and Mathematics
Teaching for Oklahoma
Rockwood Elementary School
Oklahoma City, OK

Photo Credits

3, (bkgrnd)Guy Motil/Westlight, (bl)Courtesy of the Museum of the Numismatic Association; **4,** (l)Victor Boswell/National Geographic Society, (c)Courtesy of the Museum of the Numismatic Association, (r)Edward S. Curtis/National Geographic Society; **5,** (tl)(lc)Charles O'Rear/Westlight, (tr)(br)Courtesy of the Museum of the Numismatic Association; **8,** Courtesy of the Museum of the Numismatic Association; **9,** (c)Guy Motil/Westlight, (br)Courtesy of the Museum of the Numismatic Association; **10,** Official U.S. Mint photograph; **11,** (l)Nicholas DeSciose/Photo Researchers, (r)Bryan F. Peterson/The Stock Market; **12,** (tr)(rc)Archive Photos, (bl)Courtesy of the Museum of the Numismatic Association; **13,** (tr)(br)(bl)Courtesy of the Museum of the Numismatic Association, (c)David Barker/Ohio Historical Society; **14-15,** (bkgrnd)Guy Motil/Westlight, (lc)(b)(t)(tr)(c)Courtesy of the Museum of the Numismatic Association; **16,** (bl)From The World Book Encyclopedia.©1995 World Book, Inc. By permission of the publisher., (br)Tom McHugh/Photo Researchers; **17, 18,** From The World Book Encyclopedia.©1995 World Book, Inc. By permission of the publisher.; **18,** (bl)(c)Official U.S. Mint photograph; **19,** (tl)(c)(bl)(br)Official U.S. Mint photograph, (rc)Jim Amos/Photo Researchers; **20, 21, 25, 29, 30,** Courtesy of the Museum of the Numismatic Association; **23,** (tr)Courtesy of the Museum of the Numismatic Association, (br)Aaron Haupt/SRA/McGraw-Hill; **24, 26, 27,** Aaron Haupt/SRA/McGraw-Hill; **28-29,** (bkgrnd)Phototone; **31,** Lambert/Archive Photos.

Illustration Credits

Cover, Jim Deal; **3, 6, 7, 10, 13, 14, 15, 17, 18, 23, 28, 29, 30, 31,** Steve McInturff; **8, 9,** Jim McGinness; **9, 20, 21,** Jeff Kobelt; **16, 17, 18, 19,** John Edwards and Associates.

Table of Contents

ONE CENT

This coin is more than 134 years old! They don't make them like they used to.

1932

25¢

What I$ Money?

What do you think of when you hear the word *money*? A dollar bill? A stack of quarters? Actually, anything that you can trade for something else is money. People have used money that may seem very strange to most of us.

Shells were one of the first forms of money. The Chinese used cowrie shells. Native Americans also used shells. They strung them, along with beads they made, into belts they called *wampum*.

Salt was another popular money. Africans, Ethiopians, Romans, and the Chinese traded lumps of salt for other things they needed.

Some people traded food and other plants. In Mexico **cacao beans** were used as money.

Colonial Americans used **tobacco leaves** as money.

In Newfoundland people used **dried codfish.** Imagine carrying that around in your pocket!

People on the island of Santa Cruz used the lightest money—**red feathers.**

The heaviest money we know of came from Yap. People traded **huge stone rings** that were 12 feet tall and weighed 500 pounds each.

People started making and using **coins** thousands of years ago. Nobody knows for sure when the first coins were made. Some people believe coins were used in Mesopotamia about 5,000 years ago. Others think the first coins were made in Lydia (now Turkey) about 2,600 years ago. The Greeks were probably using coins about that same time.

Greeks had the smallest pieces of money— they were about the size of apple seeds.

They called them **obelas.** People carried them in their mouths so they wouldn't lose them.

Lydian gold staters

Athens silver tetradrachm

Nails were valuable in Colonial America. Colonists building a new home might burn down the old one just to get the nails back.

Whenever that first coin was made and used, whoever made it, it led to those shiny round pieces of metal we like to have in our pockets today.

If Coins Could Talk

Good, it's quiet again. All that bouncing and clanging around was wearing me out.

What are you babbling about?

Oh, I was just saying how I've been moved from place to place to place, and I'm tired.

Well, get used to it. Before you're through, you'll have a lot of miles on you. A lot of scratches, a lot of wear and tear.

How do you know?

Look at me. I'm old. And I've been around, kid. Check out my date. I came from the Denver Mint, which everybody knows is the best, in 1932. I've helped buy everything from a pack of gum to a ride on a merry-go-round to a cordless telephone. I've been in jukeboxes, parking meters, and candy machines.

One time I was in a guy's pocket when he flew in a plane to Mexico. He traded me for a peso and left me there. Of course, I made it home eventually. But I had some fun while I was away. I've had plenty of adventures. Once a kid accidentally dropped me through the bleachers at a football game. It was months before one of the maintenance men came along with a metal detector and found me. Once I belonged to a girl who used me in her magic tricks. We fooled everybody. One minute I was there; the next minute I was gone. It was a hoot. Nobody ever figured out where I was hiding.

That's great! Sounds like I've got a lot to look forward to. Maybe all that jostling around is worth it.

Yes, because the average life of a penny is 30 years!

United States Mints

A mint is a place where metal coins are made. There are four United States Mints operating today. They are in Philadelphia, Pennsylvania; Denver, Colorado; San Francisco, California; and West Point, New York. The part of government called the Department of the Treasury runs all United States Mints.

The first U.S. Mint was built in Philadelphia in 1792. At that time, Philadelphia was the nation's capital. As the nation grew, so did coin production. To keep up, the mint moved three times—always to a larger building. The current building (the fourth one) opened in 1969. It has 500,000 square feet of space.

The **Philadelphia Mint** is full of special exhibits. A series of beautiful mosaics lines the lobby walls. Each scene shows how ancient coins were made. In the tour gallery, there's a huge map that shows locations of every U.S. Mint, past and present. You can also see Peter the Eagle here. In the 1800s, Peter lived in the mint. Most people think he was the model for the eagle on our coins today. When Peter died, workers at the mint were very sad and didn't want to let him go. So they had his body stuffed and mounted.

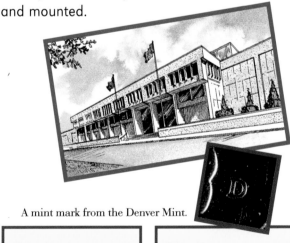

The letter near the date on a coin is the mint mark. It indicates where the coin was minted.

A mint mark from the Denver Mint.

Mints Past and Present

CC Carson City, Nevada	**C** Charlotte, North Carolina	**D** Dahlonega, Georgia	**D** Denver, Colorado
1870-1893	**1838-1861** (gold coins only)	**1838-1861** (gold coins only)	**1906-present**

The **San Francisco Mint** opened in 1852. The newest building opened in the summer of 1937. It has 33,000 square feet of space. Between 1955 and the mid-1960s, the San Francisco operation was not a mint, but an assay office. That means it did not produce coins. It melted gold, tested it for purity, poured it into bars, and stamped each bar with its weight and fineness (purity).

Since 1968, the San Francisco Mint has produced all our proof coins. Proof coins are made especially for collectors. They're polished until they have a shiny, mirror-like surface. They don't go into circulation, so they don't get scratched, worn down, or dirty.

The **West Point Mint** was completed in 1938. Originally it was the main storehouse of United States silver. It also stored one-fourth of the nation's gold. No coins were produced there until 1974, when there was a shortage of pennies. That year the West Point Mint made one billion pennies.

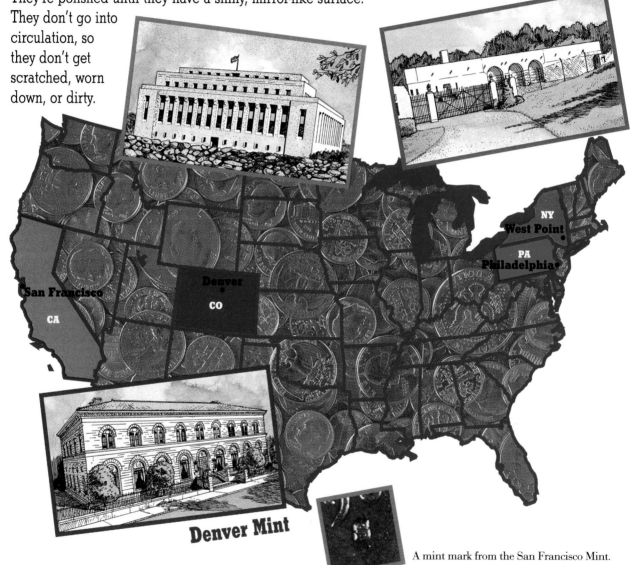

Denver Mint

A mint mark from the San Francisco Mint.

0 New Orleans, Louisiana	**P** Philadelphia, Pennsylvania	**S** San Francisco, California	**W** West Point, New York
1838-1861 & 1879-1909	**1793-present**	**1854-1955 & 1968-present**	**1984-present** (gold coins only)

The Denver Mint

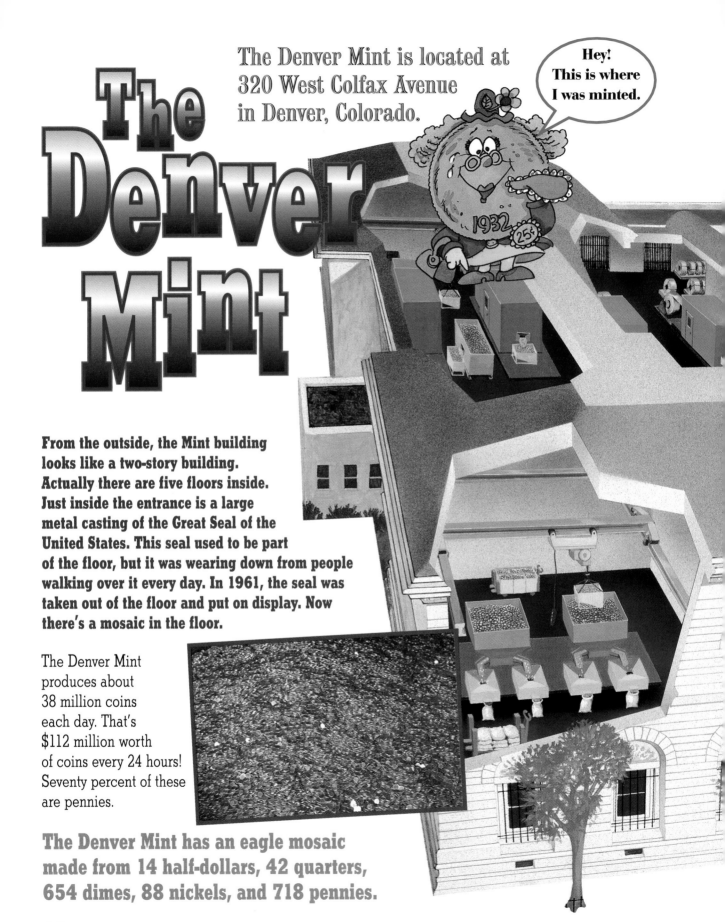

The Denver Mint is located at 320 West Colfax Avenue in Denver, Colorado.

Hey! This is where I was minted.

From the outside, the Mint building looks like a two-story building. Actually there are five floors inside. Just inside the entrance is a large metal casting of the Great Seal of the United States. This seal used to be part of the floor, but it was wearing down from people walking over it every day. In 1961, the seal was taken out of the floor and put on display. Now there's a mosaic in the floor.

The Denver Mint produces about 38 million coins each day. That's $112 million worth of coins every 24 hours! Seventy percent of these are pennies.

The Denver Mint has an eagle mosaic made from 14 half-dollars, 42 quarters, 654 dimes, 88 nickels, and 718 pennies.

The Mint has 70 coin-making machines. Fifty are older machines that can produce about 450 coins per minute. The other 20 are newer, computer-operated machines that can produce about 850 coins per minute.

The Denver Mint is a large gold depository. Gold is stored there for safekeeping. Six gold bars are on display for visitors to see. An average bar weighs $27\frac{1}{2}$ pounds.

Visitors to the Denver Mint can make their own medal on a machine called a Mint Standard Press. The machine was originally used to make dimes in the Philadelphia Mint. In 1965 it was moved to Denver, then in 1967 to San Francisco, and to Florida in 1976. Finally it moved back to Denver to produce Gold Colorado Centennial Medals. Today it is especially for visitors who stamp their own Denver Mint Souvenir Medal.

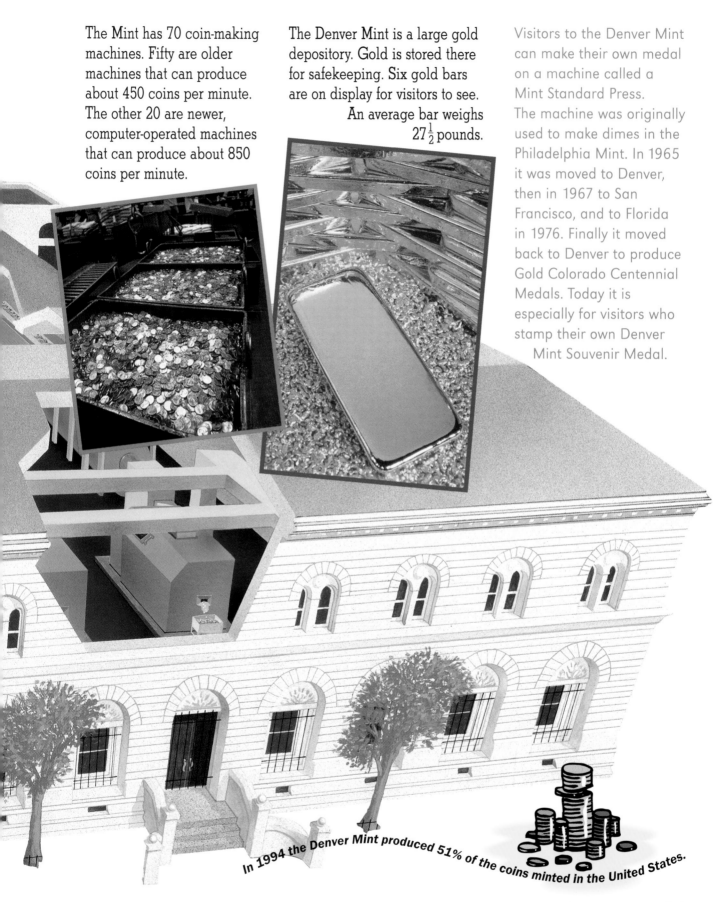

In 1994 the Denver Mint produced 51% of the coins minted in the United States.

History of the Denver Mint

The Colorado Gold Rush started near Denver in 1858. As miners found more and more gold, private mints and assay offices were built to handle it all. In 1861 the U.S. government decided that private mints could no longer operate. In 1863 a U.S. Assay Office opened in Denver. Miners brought their gold in for testing, weighing, and stamping, and had it melted into bars.

Silver was discovered in the area in 1872, and the Assay Office processed that, too. Finally, in 1895, Congress approved a U.S. Mint office in Denver for making silver and gold coins. Building began in 1899.

The Denver Mint opened for business in 1906. That year, it produced gold coins worth $23.8 million. It also produced $3.2 million in half-dollars, quarters, and dimes. In 1911 workers at the Mint started making five-cent and one-cent pieces. Before that, only the Philadelphia Mint could make those coins.

Colorado silver ore

12

Mint officials learned something from early miners who scooped dirt into a pan and then washed the dirt out, leaving the heavier gold nuggets in the pan. The Mint used to save all its dirt. Workers swept up every speck, bagged it, and stored it in a special sweeps cellar. The sweeps also contained tiny flecks of gold, silver, nickel, and copper from the floor and machines of the Mint. When the sweeps cellar filled up, the bags of dirt and precious metal flecks were sold to the highest bidder. The Mint made about $25,000 a year from selling its sweeps.

The Mint building has been expanded three times. In 1937 builders added 6,000 square feet. In 1945 a three-story structure that was 161 feet long by 96 feet wide was added. A visitors' balcony was also built so people could watch the coin-making process. The latest improvements started in 1984. They included a two-story addition, improvement of the south dock and roadways, and new equipment.

Colorado gold Clark Gruber 20-dollar coin

California 1849 coin

California fractional gold 1855 quarter-dollar

How much is a million dollars? A stack of pennies 95 miles high, a school bus full of nickels, or a pile of quarters that weighs as much as a whale.

California gold Kellog & Co. 1854 20-dollar coin

It seems like only yesterday that I was a new coin.

Mint Services

Collector Coins

Mints produce proof sets and commemorative coins for sale to the public.

Commemorative coins mark special occasions, people, and places. Money raised from selling these special coins helps pay for special events. The Olympic coins made in 1983 and 1984 helped to pay for the Olympic Games in Los Angeles. The Statue of Liberty coins made in 1986 helped pay to restore the famous statue. Civil War Commemoratives made in 1995 helped pay for the preservation of Civil War battlefields.

Most proof and commemorative coins come from the Mints in San Francisco and West Point.

Foreign Coins

In the past, U.S. Mints made coins for friendly foreign governments. Between 1875 and 1984, they produced 11,325,756,346 foreign coins.

In 1906 the Denver Mint produced 4.8 million 5-peso gold pieces for Mexico.

In 1944 and 1945 the San Francisco Mint produced coins for the Philippine Islands.

In 1975 and 1977 the Mint at West Point produced bronze 1-centesimo coins for Panama.

No foreign coins have been produced by U.S. Mint facilities since 1984.

Medals

The Philadelphia and Denver Mints make medals. These medals honor people for special accomplishments, exceptional courage, and public service. At the Philadelphia Mint, you can watch medals being made.

Since 1776 about 300 people—including George Washington, John Wayne, Lady Bird Johnson, Joe Louis, and Charles Lindbergh—have received Congressional Gold Medals. You can see bronze copies of these medals at the Philadelphia Mint.

The Mint makes miniature presidential medals especially for kids who want to collect them.

Tours

The public is welcome to tour the Philadelphia Mint, the Denver Mint, and the San Francisco Old Mint. Admission is free.

The Philadelphia Mint is open from 9 A.M. to 3:30 P.M., but the days vary by season.

The Denver Mint is open Monday through Friday from 8 A.M. to 3 P.M. (summer) or 8:30 A.M. to 3 P.M. (winter).

The San Francisco Old Mint is open Monday through Friday from 10 A.M. to 3 P.M.

How does a vending machine know which coins you put in it? It "reads" each coin to find the weight, size, thickness, and electrical properties of the metals.

How Coins Are Made

We know what coins are, and we know that they're made in a Mint. But *how* is a coin made?

The making of a coin really starts with an artist. The artist sketches one or more designs for a coin. (Sometimes more than one artist works on the sketches.) The Director of the Mint and the Secretary of the Treasury choose the two sketches they will use—one for each side of the coin.

Once the sketches are approved, the artist sculpts a model of the coin out of clay or a special plastic wax. This model has to be big enough that every tiny detail is clear—usually 3 to 12 times bigger than the finished coin will be.

Next the model is covered with plaster of paris. After the plaster dries and turns hard, the artist pulls it off the model. The plaster is a reverse of the model. The artist checks every detail to make sure the mold is perfect.

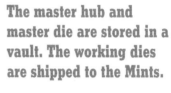

From the plaster mold, the artist makes a rubber and epoxy model. This model is mounted on a machine called a *transfer-engraver.* At one end of the transfer-engraver, a stylus traces the model. The tracing is reduced, or made smaller. At the other end of the machine, a strong cutting tool cuts the reduced design into a piece of soft steel the size of the finished coin. This is called the *master hub.*

Another machine makes a copy of the master hub called a *master die.* Then copies of the master die are made. These copies are called *working dies* because they will actually do the work of stamping new coins.

The master hub and master die are stored in a vault. The working dies are shipped to the Mints.

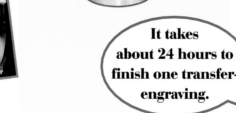

It takes about 24 hours to finish one transfer-engraving.

Now for the actual production...

Here's a look at the workings of the Denver Mint.

Long strips of metal arrive from manufacturers. The strips are 13 inches wide and 1,500 feet long. These strips go through a machine that punches out coin-sized blanks. The blanks are plain on both sides.

Screens called *riddlers* are used to sort out imperfect blanks. Blanks that are thin or incomplete fall through the screen. Imperfect blanks are melted down and used again.

The good blanks are heated in an annealing furnace. The heat softens them and makes it easier for the dies to stamp them. This helps keep the dies from wearing down too quickly.

After heating, the blanks run through a special washer and dryer.

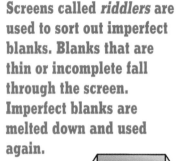

The "head" side of a coin is known as the obverse side.

The "tail" side is called the reverse.

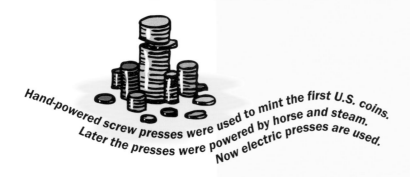

Hand-powered screw presses were used to mint the first U.S. coins. Later the presses were powered by horse and steam. Now electric presses are used.

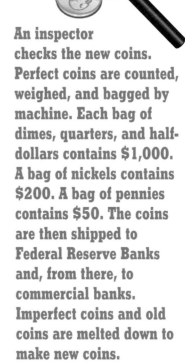

An inspector checks the new coins. Perfect coins are counted, weighed, and bagged by machine. Each bag of dimes, quarters, and half-dollars contains $1,000. A bag of nickels contains $200. A bag of pennies contains $50. The coins are then shipped to Federal Reserve Banks and, from there, to commercial banks. Imperfect coins and old coins are melted down to make new coins.

The blanks now go into a coining press where two working dies stamp the designs—one die on each side of the coin. If dimes or quarters are being stamped, their edges are reeded—ridged— at the same time.

The blanks go into a milling or upsetting machine that puts a raised rim around each one.

Could Be Silver, Could Be an Alloy

Through the years coin denominations have come and gone. The $10 gold piece, the three-cent piece, the two-cent piece, and the half-cent are examples. Weights and metal content have changed also. These pie graphs show some changes through the years.

88%

12%

0.16345 ounce

Indian Head cent prior to 1864

Lincoln Head cent prior to 1982

0.10885 ounce

5%

95%

1994 Lincoln Head cent

97.5%

2.5%

0.0875 ounce

Key

copper
nickel
silver
tin and zinc
zinc

The five-cent piece was established in 1866. Except for during World War II, it has had the same metal composition and weight since 1883. From 1942–1945 the five-cent piece was made up of 56% copper, 35% silver, and 9% manganese.

75%
25%

0.175 ounce

1994 Jefferson five-cent piece

89.24%

10.76%

0.0945 ounce

1796 dime

Metal content is the same for half-dimes, quarters, and half-dollars of the same time period.

90%
10%

0.0875 ounce

1873 dime

1994 dime

outer layer

25%
75%

inner core

100%

0.07938 ounce

Metal content is the same for quarters of the same time period.

New Miss Mattix

Actually the word is *numismatics*. It means collecting and studying coins. Numismatics is very popular. In 1850 there were about 300 coin collectors in the United States. Today there are more than 20 million.

How to Start a Coin Collection

1
Start with the change in your purse or pocket. You probably won't find any rare coins this way, but you can still begin a nice collection. Use a metal detector to find coins for your collection.

2
Order coins through the mail. You can also order proof sets directly from the San Francisco Mint.

3
Buy coins from a dealer. Look in the Yellow Pages for names, addresses, and phone numbers. Dealers are also a good source of information. Ask questions to learn more.

4
Go to a coin show. This is a good place to learn.

5
Join a coin club if there's one in your area. This way you can learn from other members, share interesting finds, and even trade coins.

6
Visit your library and bookstore; both have books and magazines especially for coin lovers.

The Philadelphia Mint mark appears only on Jefferson five-cent pieces issued between 1942 and 1945 and on other coins minted after 1979.

Grades for Coins

Proof perfect

Uncirculated shows no wear

Extremely fine shows only a little wear on the highest points of the design

Very fine shows a little wear overall, all details are clear

Fine much of the details are worn away, all lettering is clear

Very good shows a lot of wear on main features, but has no big gouges or scratches

Good main parts of the design are still distinguishable, but coin is very worn

Fair extremely worn and of little or no value to a collector

Proof

Fair

Seated Liberty 25 cent coins

Taking Care of Your Coins

- Pick up coins by their edges only. Your fingers can damage coins enough to lower their value.

- Never clean a coin. This often lowers the value, and rarely increases the value of a coin.

- Never allow coins to bump together. This can scratch or nick the surfaces of the coins.

- Never use rubber bands or regular paper to hold or wrap coins in. These contain substances that can tarnish coins.

- Store your coins in coin albums or coin boards made especially for this purpose. Coin boards can help you focus on a certain type of collection. You can see what you need at a glance. Plastic holders made for one coin, clear plastic envelopes, clear plastic tubes, and tarnish-free paper are also available for storing coins.

Look at me!

1987-D
4.9 BILLION

1988
6.1 BILLION

1990
6.9 BILLION

1990-D
4.9 BILLION

1992-D

1993

1993-D

1995

Look Very Carefully

Examining coins can be very interesting. Take a look at these coins produced by the Denver Mint.

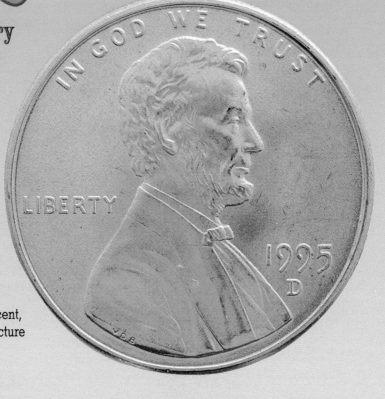

Lincoln Cent
Obverse

- **IN GOD WE TRUST.** The Act of 1955 requires this on every U.S. coin.
- **LIBERTY.** The Act of 1792 requires this on every U.S. coin.
- Portrait of Abraham Lincoln. The Lincoln cent, first issued in 1909, was the first coin to picture a real person.
- The designer's initials. VDB stands for Victor David Brenner.
- Mint mark. The D indicates coins minted in Denver.
- Date. The Act of 1792 requires this on every U.S. coin.

Reverse

- **UNITED STATES OF AMERICA.** The Act of 1792 requires this on the reverse of gold and silver coins. Those coins are no longer produced for circulation, but the words remain on all U.S. coins.
- **E PLURIBUS UNUM.** The Act of 1873 requires this motto. It means "One Out of Many."
- Picture of the Lincoln Memorial. This first appeared on the reverse of the Lincoln cent in 1959.
- The designer's initials. FG stands for Frank Gasparro.
- **ONE CENT.** The Act of 1792 requires that the reverse of all coins be stamped with their denomination.

Jefferson Five-cent Piece

Obverse

- **IN GOD WE TRUST**
- **LIBERTY**
- Portrait of Thomas Jefferson
- The designer's initials. FS stands for Felix Schlag.
- Date
- Mint mark

In 1938 a public contest was held for the best five-cent piece design. There were 395 entries. The winner got $1,000.

Some people think it's lucky to find a penny and pick it up.

Reverse

- **E PLURIBUS UNUM**
- Picture of Monticello, Jefferson's home
- **FIVE CENTS**
- **UNITED STATES OF AMERICA**

The words *penny* and *nickel* are really slang terms. Penny comes from the pence, a British coin used by the American colonists.

Twenty-five percent of the metal in five-cent pieces is nickel, so people just started calling them nickels.

Roosevelt Dime

Obverse

- **IN GOD WE TRUST**
- **LIBERTY**
- Portrait of Franklin Delano Roosevelt
- The designer's initials. JS stands for John Sinnock.
- Mint mark
- Date

Reverse

- **UNITED STATES OF AMERICA**
- **E PLURIBUS UNUM**
- **ONE DIME**
- Olive branch symbolizing peace
- Torch, which stands for liberty
- Oak branch, which stands for strength and independence

The first Roosevelt dime was released on January 30, 1946.

Washington Quarter

Obverse

- **LIBERTY**
- **IN GOD WE TRUST**
- Portrait of George Washington
- Date
- Mint mark

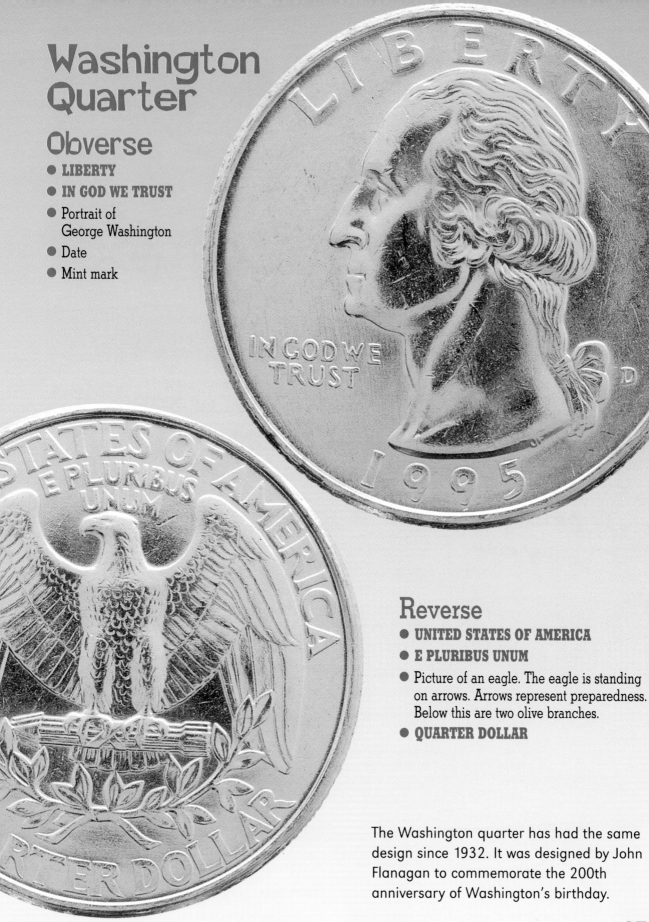

Reverse

- **UNITED STATES OF AMERICA**
- **E PLURIBUS UNUM**
- Picture of an eagle. The eagle is standing on arrows. Arrows represent preparedness. Below this are two olive branches.
- **QUARTER DOLLAR**

The Washington quarter has had the same design since 1932. It was designed by John Flanagan to commemorate the 200th anniversary of Washington's birthday.

¢ents and Nonsense

Everyday expressions and fascinating facts about money . . .

In 1994 the U.S. Mints produced 13.6 billion pennies, 1.4 billion nickels, 2.5 billion dimes, 1.7 billion quarters, and 47.5 million half-dollars.

mint condition

dime a dance

pass the buck

a penny saved is a penny earned

penny ante

The two-cent piece was not popular and was discontinued after only nine years.

a million-dollar smile

put your money where your mouth is

the buck stops here

worth your weight in gold

During World War II, nickel and copper were badly needed for the war effort, so nickel was taken out of the five-cent piece, and copper pennies were not made. In 1943 a steel cent was made, and in 1944 a bronze cent was made from used shell casings.

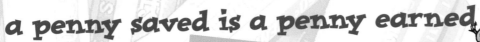

penny wise; pound foolish

don't take any wooden nickels

nickel and dime you to death

At one time or another, the United States has had a 20-cent coin, a half-cent coin, a 2-cent coin, and a 3-cent coin.

a wealth of information

In 1964 a new half-dollar replaced the one that pictured Benjamin Franklin. The new coin pictured John F. Kennedy. Half-dollars are still in circulation, but are no longer minted.

The most valuable U.S. coin is the 1870 $3 gold piece. Only one is known to exist.

dime a dozen

not worth a plugged nickel

a penny for your thoughts

you look like a million bucks

sound as a dollar

The first coin with the United States name on it (1787) also had this motto— "Mind Your Business."

stop on a dime

"Black Diamond," a buffalo at the Bronx Zoo, was the model for the 1938 buffalo nickel.

In 1792 metal for coins was scarce. Colonists donated nails, spikes, kitchen utensils, and finishings from old and wrecked ships. George Washington donated a copper kettle and a pair of tongs.

For More Information...

...you could write to

Coins Magazine
700 E. State Street
Iola, WI 54990

American Numismatic Association
818 N. Cascade Avenue
Colorado Springs, CO 80903-3279

Heritage Numismatic Auctions
Heritage Plaza
Highland Park Village
Dallas, TX 75205

Connecticut Numismatic Auctions
P.O. Box 471
Plantsville, CT 06479

Department of the Treasury
United States Mint
633 Third Street NW
Washington, DC 20220

Customer Services
U.S. Mint
10001 Aerospace Road
Lanham, MD 20706
(301) 436-7400

Philadelphia Mint
Fifth Street at Independence Mall
Philadelphia, PA 19106
(215) 597-7350

Denver Mint
Colfax and Delaware Streets
Denver, Colorado 80204
(303) 844-3582

This is the Susan B. Anthony dollar coin. It has the same value as a paper dollar bill.

or you could read

Collecting Coins for Pleasure & Profit by Barry Krause.

The How and Why Wonder Book of Coins and Currency by Paul Gelinas.

How Money Is Made by David Cooke.

The Kids' Money Book by Neale Godfrey.

Know Your Government: The U.S. Mint by Paul Wolman.

The Story of Coins by Sam Rosenfeld.

The Story of Money by Betsy Maestro.

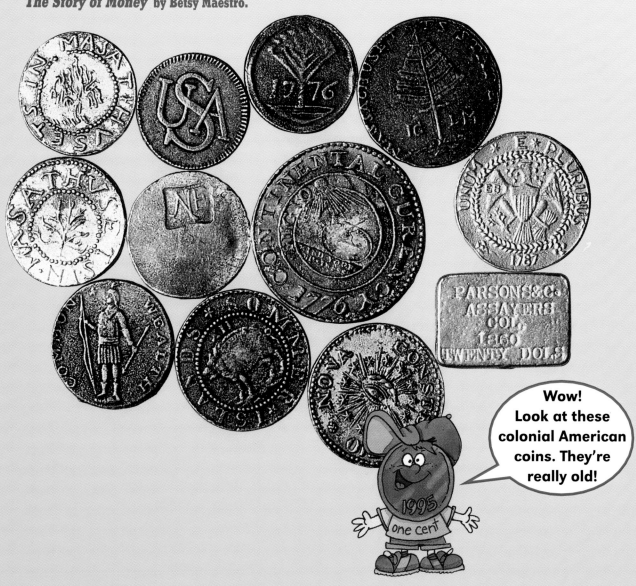

Wow! Look at these colonial American coins. They're really old!

Index